'TIS THE SEASON TO BE BAKING

'TIS THE SEASON TO BE BAKING

CHRISTMAS REFLECTIONS AND BREAD RECIPES

BY FR. DOMINIC GARRAMONE, O.S.B.

REEDY PRESS
St. Louis, Missouri

Reedy Press
PO Box 5131
St. Louis, MO 63139

Library of Congress Control Number: 2007931131

ISBN: 978-1-933370-05-7
*   1-933370-05-X*

For information on all Reedy Press publications visit our website at www.reedypress.com.

Printed in the United States of America
07 08 09 10 11   5 4 3 2 1

Dedicated to the memory of
Fr. Herbert Comyns, O.S.B.,
whose reverent observance of Advent
taught me how to wait for Christmas.

Contents

Acknowledgments

Like a well-planned Christmas celebration, a book (even one as modest as this one) requires the assistance of many hearts and hands. I wish to express my gratitude to the following "angels":

- My students Kevin Rosenberg, Andrew Loebach, and Christopher Jacobsen for their help in developing and testing recipes;
- Matt Andrew, Greg Hoffman, and Thomas Tonozzi for bearing the burden of contractual negotiations and the other kinds of business they don't teach you in the seminary;
- Josh Stevens and Matt Heidenry of Reedy Press, both of whom have been dedicated to the success of this book;
- All my families—natural, monastic, academic, and extended—for inspiring to find new ways to celebrate the birth of the Lord.

The Catholic Post, the diocese of Peoria, Illinois

Preface

One of the most common comments I hear about baking is something like this: "I don't have time to bake bread much anymore—well, except during the holidays, of course." What an amazing paradox: many people only have time to bake during what is often viewed as the busiest time of the year! But we make time for what is most important to us. What these people are really saying is: "My family's Christmas baking traditions are so important that I always make time for them."

Perhaps you are one of these people, the ones for whom Christmas baking is a priority right up there with trimming a tree, wrapping presents and attending Christmas services. Maybe cut-out cookies are your special custom, or your family expects Grandma's cinnamon rolls on Christmas morning, or perhaps you have a traditional ethnic bread that you cherish because of the history behind it. If you are one of these people, the book is definitely for you; you will recognize your family in these pages and perhaps learn something new along the way.

This book is also for those who have no particular baking customs at Christmas but would like to establish some with their families. Maybe you vaguely remember a special bread from "the old country" that your mother or great-aunt used to make, and you want to recover that tradition. Or perhaps you're looking for a way to make your Christmas preparations more meaningful, so your family can focus on the spiritual aspects of the holiday. The reflections in this book, along with the recipes that accompany them, can give you the means to create delicious dishes for your holiday table that will nourish your spirit as well.

The breads I have selected for this book are a mixture of traditional recipes and original creations. Some have been made for centuries, some I inherited from my mother or my grandmothers, others are "new traditions" of Saint Bede Abbey that have only been around since I started baking for the community. But each bread has a connection to the characters we find in the Christmas story as it is presented in the gospels of Matthew and Luke. Each bread directs us to reflect on how we can better prepare to celebrate the holy days of the Advent and Christmas seasons. I hope the recipes and reflections included here will help you reclaim some of your own heritage or create a new tradition for your family, and make your holiday baking a means of deepening your own spirituality.

'TIS THE SEASON TO BE BAKING

Chapter One

A Domestic Spirituality

Several years ago a friend of mine, knowing
how much I like to bake, sent me a vintage woman's
magazine featuring "Our Christmas Heritage Foods from
24 Mother Countries." Now, I read a lot of cookbooks
and study baking traditions the way some people
research their family tree. As a result, many of the recipes
I recognized: Scottish shortbread, Norwegian Julekake,
German stollen and Italian pannetone, the Büche de
Noel they make every year in Fr. Arthur's French class,
and the plum pudding that is featured so prominently in
Dickens' *A Christmas Carol*. But there were other foods
I'd never heard of: Swiss Spiced Honey Cakes, a poppy
seed–filled loaf from Lithuania, a Czech triple-braided
Vanocka and a simpler Swedish Saffron Braid, Hungarian
Walnut- and Almond-filled crescents, and a fish salad
from Portugal that (I must admit) I don't intend to make
anytime soon.

Although I haven't yet tried every recipe in the
magazine, reading it inspired me to reflect on my own
Christmas baking and what it means to me. I was a baker

before I became a monk, but monastic life embraces every aspect of our life together, and everyday activities become charged with meaning. The Rule of St. Benedict says that tools of monastery should be treated with the same reverence we have for the vessels of the altar. Clearly, Benedict believed that every act of service is a sacred act.

This kind of "domestic spirituality" is especially important during the holiday season, when our preparations can seem more like drudgery if we fail to see the purpose behind them. Christmas decorations and holiday foods are not an end in themselves, and neither are the family dinners and office parties for which we prepare them. Rather, our goal should be a spiritual one.

At this point, one might expect me to get out the Guilt Hammer and start taking swings at the crass commercialism and overindulgence of the Christmas celebrations of modern society. But you've probably heard that sermon already: preachers have been delivering it since colonial times. Consider one of Cotton Mather's sermons of 1712, which included this remarkable question: "Can you in your consciences think that our Holy Savior is honored by *mirth*?"

Having our religious celebrations hijacked by consumerism is nothing new (think about *weddings* as the ultimate example), and it's always a danger in a society driven largely by economic concerns. But we can more easily resist the tendency to over-consume if we are more aware of the purpose of our festivities and feasting: to recall and celebrate all that God has done for us, and to prepare to meet God in a new way.

The happy holiday meals we enjoy are best seasoned with stories from our communal and personal histories. Every year my family gathers at the abbey to celebrate Christmas on the feast of the Holy Family (more on that tradition later). Almost every year, we vote on the menu, and usually homemade pizza is the winner by a landslide! Family members contribute a rather mismatched potluck buffet, and the prayer at the beginning of the meal is just about the only formal aspect of the celebration. But at some point, someone will say, "Uncle Marty, tell Zachary about that one time you . . ." and the next thing you know, we're all gathered around the table, sharing stories about childhood exploits, departed family members, recent successes, and dreams about the future. The menu doesn't matter as much as the memories.

Ultimately, what we are remembering is how God has been at work in our lives all along, not just at Christmas. Because the Son of God took on human flesh, the entire material world is now a vehicle of grace throughout the year. Ronald Rolheiser expresses this Christmas-every-day mentality beautifully when he writes: "God takes on flesh so that every home becomes a church, every child becomes the Christ-child, and all food and drink become a sacrament" (*The Holy Longing*, Doubleday, 1999; p. 78). In this incarnational view, our holiday celebrations are a way of encountering God through our family and friends and in the food and fellowship we share.

Unfortunately, many of us do not experience Christmas in such a sacramental way. Rather than encountering God in a new way, we encounter the same old stress and frustration of too much to do in too little time. The question of simplifying Christmas or reducing holiday stress is beyond the scope of this book. However, I do recommend that sometime in July you read a copy of *Unplug the Christmas Machine* (Jo Robinson and Jean Coppock Staeheli, Harper Paperbacks, 1991) to help put some sanity back into the season. What I will say is this: choose those activities that have the most meaning for you, the ones that give you the most spiritual and emotional nourishment, and let the rest go. The reflections and recipes that follow will help you understand the meaning behind Christmas baking traditions from around the world, so you can choose ways to make your family celebration nourishing to both body and soul.

Chapter Two

Jolly Old St. Nicholas

The modern legend of Santa Claus evolved from the life of a real-life bishop of Myra in Turkey, St. Nicholas. His feast day on December 6 offers the opportunity for some lovely holiday baking traditions, as well as an opportunity gently to counteract some of the materialism and greed associated with the season.

St. Nicholas was born to wealthy Greek parents who died when he was a teenager. A devout Christian, he made use of his fortune to help the needy. For example, the tradition of hanging up stockings for Santa to fill comes from a true story of how Nicholas left gold in the stockings of the three daughters of a poor man who couldn't afford them dowries. Several stories of how he rescued children from danger earned him the reputation as the patron saint and benefactor of children. A good friend of our monastic community, Louise Carus, has written a book titled *The Real St. Nicholas: Tales of Generosity and Hope from Around the World* (Quest Books, 2002). (She also brings us special St. Nicholas breads every year!) Her book offers a St. Nicholas folktale or legend from around the world for each day in December, and reading them as a family can help restore some of the true meaning of the holiday season.

Most European countries have traditions of St. Nicholas leaving gifts for children on his feast day. One especially charming description of the Dutch customs can be found in the children's classic *Hans Brinker*, by Mary Mapes Dodge. These traditions are too rich and varied to be summarized here, but I highly recommend accessing the information at www.stnicholascenter.org, which includes extensive descriptions of the story of St. Nicholas and the customs surrounding his feast day in countries around the world. Those without Internet access should ask for help at the local library—the photos and illustrations alone are well worth the effort, and they can print out activities and coloring pages for children from the site. There are, of course, plenty of print resources available through the library as well.

There are many baking traditions associated with the feast of St. Nicholas, primarily some form of *speculaas*, a kind of spiced gingerbread cookie, often cut out in the shape of the saint, his crosier (bishop's staff) or miter (a bishop's peaked hat). In Germany and Austria, however, breads are often made in these same shapes, as well as in the form of St. Nicholas' boot. The following recipe makes a rich, soft dough that is perfect for shaping these sweet breads.

Buttermilk Sweet Dough

Take egg and mashed potatoes out of the fridge and allow to come to room temperature. (You may also use a comparable amount of instant mashed potatoes. Just follow the package instructions to make a ½-cup serving.)

In a medium-size bowl,
sprinkle yeast over buttermilk and stir to dissolve. Allow to develop for five minutes. Add sugar, egg, potatoes, butter, and salt and beat until smooth.

Add three cups of flour, one cup at a time, mixing after each addition until the flour is completely incorporated. About 2 tablespoons at a time, knead in enough of the remaining flour to make a soft, slightly sticky dough. Knead for 4 or 5 minutes, until dough is smooth and satiny. Lightly oil the surface of the dough and place it back into rinsed bowl and cover with a clean, dry towel.

Allow to rise in a warm place free from drafts until doubled, 60 to 90 minutes. Punch dough down and shape as directed.

1 pkg. active dry yeast

1 cup lukewarm buttermilk

¼ cup granulated sugar

1 egg

½ cup mashed potatoes

¼ cup of butter, melted

1 tsp. salt

3 ¾ to 4 cups all-purpose flour

1 egg, beaten with 1 Tbs. water
    for a wash (optional)

Miter and Crosier Bread

Separate out about one third of the dough. Use this one third to make a rope about 18 inches long. Coil the end to form the crosier as illustrated and lay on a lightly greased cookie sheet.

Take the remaining dough and set aside about a quarter of it. Roll out the larger piece of dough to a thickness of about ½ inch and cut it into the miter shape as illustrated (kind of like an inverted home plate).

Use the leftover dough to form a cross on top of the miter (brush the dough with a little water to make the pieces stick). Place the miter next to the crosier on the cookie sheet so they are slightly overlapping—they will grow together during rising and baking. Cover with a clean, dry cloth and let rise until doubled, about 30 minutes. If desired, brush the top of the dough with a beaten egg for a shiny, golden brown surface.

Bake on the middle rack of a preheated 375° oven for 35 to 45 minutes or until golden brown. Allow to cool on the pan for about 20 minutes before transferring to a wire rack to cool completely. You may then decorate the bread with colored frosting, sprinkles, gumdrops for jewels, etc.

St. Nicholas' Boot

On a lightly floured board or countertop, roll dough out into a long oval about a half-inch thick and shape roughly into an "L." Use a small pastry wheel or pizza cutter to cut the boot shape (use a cardboard template if you need to) and use the cutaway dough to shape a cuff and a heel for the boot as well. Use a little water as "glue" to attach the cuff and heel as illustrated.

Place the boot on a large baking sheet that has been lightly greased. Cover with a clean, dry cloth and let rise until doubled, about 30 minutes. If desired, brush the top of the dough with a beaten egg for a shiny, golden brown surface.

Bake on the middle rack of a preheated 375° oven for 35 to 45 minutes or until golden brown. Allow to cool on the pan for about 20 minutes before transferring to a wire rack to cool completely. You may use frosting to decorate the boot, add buckles, or attach candies coming out of the top. I use a light glaze made from powdered sugar and milk, and then sprinkle on black decorating sugar left over from Halloween!

Baking these shaped breads can become a cherished family tradition and a good way to begin the holiday baking season. Children love to shape dough and decorate holiday foods. But these activities are also an opportunity to tell the story of the real St. Nicholas, perhaps even to explain how he "became" Santa. You might stress the importance of generosity and compassion for the poor during this season, and make plans for how your family will care for the needy of your locality during this season. You might ask children what it is like to do good deeds in secret, without concern for "getting credit." Above all, emphasize that St. Nicholas did his good deeds out of love for Jesus, whose birthday we are preparing to celebrate.

Many years ago I read of a way by which the feast of St. Nicholas can help decrease the emphasis on getting presents on Christmas Day. A couple had the custom of giving their children their "big" gift—bicycle, stereo, etc.—on the feast of St. Nicholas. Then on Christmas morning, they received small treats in their stockings, as well as some simpler gifts like new clothes or books. They were surprised to discover that it in no way diminished their children's enjoyment of Christmas, and in fact enhanced it by defusing the huge buildup that always seemed to end with a glut of presents followed by a vague sense of disappointment. The family members were able to make Christmas more about Christ and less about themselves.

Chapter Three

"Behold a Rose of Judah"

The season of Advent has a special emphasis on our Blessed Mother, and early in the Advent season we celebrate two feasts of our Lady: the Immaculate Conception on December 8 and Our Lady of Guadalupe on December 12.

The gospel for the solemnity of the Immaculate Conception is the story of the Annunciation, which is presented in the gospel of Luke. The angel announces to Mary that she has been chosen for a special vocation, a unique role in God's plan of salvation. At first she is uncertain: "How can this be?" But the angel assures her that nothing is impossible with God.

We ought to remember an important detail about Mary's vocation that we don't always notice in the reading. At the end of the passage, the text says, "Then the angel departed from her" (Luke 1:38). And we should add to that: *never to return*. Mary gets one moment of blazing clarity, when the Lord comes to her in a special way, and that's it—no more angels, no more visions, no more special favors from God. What she gets is what the rest of us get. She gets the experience of being with her Son, hearing his gospel and witnessing his ministry, and not always understanding. She receives revelations from her husband and visits from shepherds and the Magi and prophecies from Simeon, and she must ponder them in her heart in order to penetrate their meaning. Nonetheless, she remains faithful to her son from Bethlehem to Nazareth, from the way of the cross to Golgotha and the tomb. And so she shares in the overwhelming joy of the resurrection and the powerful flames of Pentecost.

Mary's experience mirrors our own. Few of us receive extraordinary revelations from God, and if we do, they are singular events—one special moment of clarity in a lifetime of questioning. For the most part, we must receive God's message in ordinary ways: from reading and hearing the Scriptures; from listening to the insights of our family and friends; from meditation on the events of life and pondering their meaning. Advent and Christmas are the ideal times to slow down and listen to these "angels."

The feast of Our Lady of Guadalupe commemorates Mary's appearance to Juan Diego, and the miracles accompanying his vision. When challenged by his bishop to provide proof that his vision was true, Juan was directed by Mary to gather roses growing out of season on the hillside. He filled his peasant's cloak with blooms, and when they tumbled out before the astonished bishop, Mary's image was found on the inside of his cloak.

Roses have been associated with Mary for centuries. In hymns and litanies she is referred to as "the Rose of Judah" and "the Mystical Rose." So it is appropriate that Rose Rolls should be one of our bread recipes for Advent and Christmas. These beautiful breads are formed much like cinnamon rolls: the dough is rolled out into a rectangle and spread with butter, then rolled into a spiral. The rolls are cut and laid cut side down into muffin tins, and a cross is cut into each with a sharp scissors. As they rise before and during baking, the rolls unfurl into petals. It's a simple technique, but the results are quite spectacular and make you look like a professional pastry chef!

Aside from their beautiful aroma, flavor, and appearance, Rose Rolls have their own spiritual message: they take their shape only because the cross has been cut into them. Mary's willingness to share in the cross of her Son transformed her from simple maiden of Nazareth into the Rose of Judah, bringing the fulfillment of the promises made to the people of Israel. Our own share in the cross unites us with Mary and all the saints in the Mystical Rose, the symbol of paradise and of the eternal unity with Christ that is our destiny.

Rose Rolls

Use any dough recipe that will make a dozen dinner rolls, preferably one that uses milk and eggs to enrich the dough. The recipe for Holiday Bread on page 71 yields enough for two dozen rolls.

On a lightly floured board, roll dough out into a rectangle 12 inches high by 15 inches wide. Brush the dough with the melted butter, leaving 1 inch of the top edge dry. Roll the dough up jellyroll style. Lightly brush the top edge with a little water, so it will stick to the roll; pinch to seal.

Using a sharp knife, cut the roll into 12 even pieces. Cut side down, place them one by one into the cups of a lightly greased muffin tin. Using a pair of scissors, cut an "X" in the top of each roll—you should cut about $\frac{2}{3}$ of the way through the roll. Cover and let rise in a warm place until doubled, about 30 minutes.

Bake in a preheated 375° oven for 10 to 12 minutes, or until lightly browned. Remove from pans and place on wire racks to cool slightly. If desired, brush tops of rolls with more melted butter before serving warm.

Chapter Four

"And Joseph Went Up to Bethlehem"

There is an ancient custom in Hungary and Croatia to offer green sprouts of new wheat to the Infant in the manger. As with so many Christmas traditions, it began as a pagan custom. People would sow wheat in a cup or dish on December 13 (which was, in the Julian Calendar, the longest night of the year). If the wheat grew thick and high by December 24, it meant prosperity in the coming year. As Christian culture began to "baptize" pagan superstitions, the tradition took on a new meaning.

The wheat seeds are still planted on December 13, now known as the feast of St. Lucy, and are symbolic of the offering of the agricultural year that is to begin in the spring. On Christmas Eve the green sprouts are placed as an offering at the Nativity scene, either in the home or at the church.

The wheat at the manger can also remind us that the birth of the child is also the birth of the one who will declare "I am the bread of life" (John 6:35). Indeed, the place-name "Bethlehem" means "house of bread," and the infant Jesus is placed in a manger where grain would usually be placed for feed. It is no coincidence that every culture and ethnicity of Christendom developed special breads to celebrate Christmas. As we enjoy them at the family table, we are reminded of the *panis angelicus*, the bread of angels prefigured by the manna in the desert and brought to fulfillment in the Eucharist.

You can grow your own offering of Christmas wheat in a 4- or 5-inch flower pot filled with new potting soil. Place the seeds just below the surface of the soil and keep the soil moist but not soaking in a sunny location. You might use an indoor grow light if you have one, but a southeastern window will do just as well. The sprouts should be 6 to 8 inches tall by Christmas Eve. The wheat may also be used as a table decoration by growing the sprouts in a ring-shaped container—a decorative copper jello mold works beautifully—and then placing a candle in the center.

Christmas wheat sprouting

Lighted candles feature prominently in another custom for the feast of St. Lucy, one originating in Sweden. The oldest daughter of a family will wake up before dawn on St. Lucy's Day and dress in a white gown symbolic of Lucy's virginity, often with a red sash as a sign of the saint's martyrdom. On her head she will wear a wreath of greenery with several lit candles. If she has younger brothers, she may be accompanied by "starboys," dressed in white gowns and cone-shaped hats decorated with gold stars, and carrying star-tipped wands. "Santa Lucia" will go around the house to awaken the family and serve them saffron buns and hot coffee. Throughout the day, girls visit hospitals, factories, and offices with their treats. The buns may be the usual round shape, but they are more traditionally shaped into X's, figure eights, S-shapes, or crowns. They are also called *Lussekatter*, St. Lucia's Cats. (See the website www.luciamorning.com for more information and illustrations.)

A Note about Saffron

Saffron is an extremely expensive spice. It comes from the stigmas of a species of crocus, and pound for pound is more expensive than gold. A jar with only three stigmas (called "threads") costs over $10 in most grocery stores, if you can find it at all. But a little bit goes a long way, and it adds a lovely golden color to these rolls. If you can afford it, try using real saffron for this recipe. You can substitute a half teaspoon of ground cardamom (another traditional spice for Swedish breads and cakes) or turmeric with a drop or two of yellow food coloring to the dough.

St. Lucia Buns (Lussekatter)

2 pkg. active dry yeast

2 cups lukewarm milk (about 100 to 110°)

½ cup granulated sugar

½ tsp. powdered saffron

1 tsp. salt

½ cup (1 stick) of butter, melted

5 ½ to 6 cups of all-purpose flour

1 beaten egg

raisins for decoration

In a medium-size bowl, dissolve yeast in milk and let stand for five minutes. Add sugar, saffron, and salt and stir until thoroughly blended. Stir in butter; then add 5 cups flour about one cup at a time, mixing each cup until it is thoroughly incorporated.

Turn dough out onto a lightly floured board and knead for 5 or 6 minutes, adding small amounts of flour to keep the dough manageable. You should end up with dough that is smooth but still soft and only slightly sticky. Lightly oil the surface of the dough and place it in a clean bowl in a warm place free of drafts; cover with a clean cloth or towel. Let rise for 90 minutes or until doubled in bulk.

Punch dough down and knead for about 3 minutes to expel large pockets of air. Divide dough into 24 pieces. Roll each piece into a rope about 10 inches long and shape into a curled "S" or a figure eight. Place rolls on lightly greased cookie sheets (do not crowd them together) and cover with a clean, dry cloth. Let rise until nearly doubled in bulk, about 30 minutes.

Preheat oven to 475°. Brush rolls gently with beaten egg and decorate the curls with the raisins. Bake until golden brown, about 15 to 20 minutes. Cool on racks.

Both the wheat traditions of Eastern Europe
and Sweden's festival of light are reminders that Jesus'
birth is the herald of the end of the long winter night of
sin, which is celebrated in the texts used in Christian
tradition in every nation:

> From this day,
> night decreases, day increases,
> darkness is shaken, light grows longer,
> and the loss of night shall make the gain of day.
> *From a seventh-century Irish antiphon for Christmas*

> Light and salvation are now born to us,
> night is driven away,
> and death is vanquished:
> Oh! Come all ye people, believe:
> God is born of Mary.
> *From a sequence by Venatius Fortunatus, Northern Italy*

> Christ is the morning star,
> who when the night of this world is past
> brings to his saints
> the promise of the light of life
> and opens everlasting day.
> *From the writings of St. Bede, Northumbria England*

This last text (which is inscribed above Bede's tomb in
Durham Cathedral) points to an even more hope-filled
promise. Christmas marks the beginning of the growing

light here on earth, in the cycle of the seasons—but it points to that infinitely greater light of eternal life, which is promised to those who persevere to the end, when the darkness of death will be vanquished forever. Our Christmas feasting is but a foretaste of the eternal wedding feast in heaven, described so eloquently by the prophet Isaiah:

> On this mountain the LORD of hosts
>   will provide for all peoples
> A feast of rich food and choice wines,
>   juicy, rich food and pure, choice wines.
> On this mountain he will destroy
>   the veil that veils all peoples,
> The web that is woven over all nations;
>   he will destroy death forever.
> The Lord GOD will wipe away
>   the tears from all faces;
> The reproach of his people he will remove
>   from the whole earth;
>   for the LORD has spoken.
>   (Isaiah 25:6-8)

Chapter Five

"Of the House and Lineage of David"

At the end of Advent, we come to the Mass on the evening of December 24—the evening Mass that is still part of the Advent season, not the midnight vigil of Christmas. The gospel reading of this Mass is the birth narrative in the gospel of Matthew that begins with the genealogy of Jesus (Mt 1:1-17). The purpose of this long list of names is not merely to establish the biological or legal lineage of Jesus. Rather, it is the means by which Matthew establishes that Jesus is indeed an anointed "Son of David" and therefore may be called "Messiah" or "Christ."

The Christmas bread that best represents the genealogy of Jesus is called fougasse, served at a traditional French meal known as *Le Reveillon.* Reveillon is a very late supper held after Midnight Mass on Christmas Eve. The menu for the meal varies according to regional culinary tradition. In Alsace, goose is the main course; in Burgundy, it's turkey accompanied by chestnuts; while wealthy Parisians feast upon oysters, lobster, and paté de foie gras. It is traditional in Provence to end the reveillon with thirteen desserts symbolizing Christ and the twelve apostles. Some kind of fougasse is usually served, sweet or savory. The following recipe uses onions and walnuts for an interesting flavor and texture, but I've also made fougasse with a sweet dough with dried fruits and toasted almonds mixed in.

I usually cut my fougasse into the "Tree of Life" shape (see illustration) as a reminder of the genealogy of Jesus, depicted in medieval manuscripts as the "tree of Jesse." The idea of depicting the ancestors of Jesus as the branches of a tree comes from Isaiah 11, one of the Immanual predictions. The chapter begins:

> But a shoot shall sprout from the stump of Jesse,
>> and from his roots a bud shall blossom.
> The spirit of the LORD shall rest upon him:
>> a spirit of wisdom and of understanding,
> A spirit of counsel and of strength,
>> a spirit of knowledge and of fear of the LORD,
>> and his delight shall be the fear of the LORD.
> (Isaiah 11:1-3)

Thus the Messiah is a shoot from the stump of Jesse, even though it seemed that the line of David had been cut off. Matthew's genealogy traces the history of that line, beginning with Abraham and ending with Joseph, Mary, and Jesus.

The genealogy of Jesus contains a remarkable array of characters: revered patriarchs and unknown ancestors, faithful kings and idolatrous despots, adulterers, prostitutes, foreigners, penitents and reprobates, and ordinary believers. Stephen J. Binz makes an insightful assessment of the meaning of this text:

> God works in peculiar ways. The genealogy gives us a preview of that peculiar collection of men and women who will follow Jesus and will become the Church in which Matthew ministered. The sinful, scandalous, unknown, and marginalized people who will come into the kingdom and experience salvation in Christ are powerful witnesses that the Holy Spirit is at work.
> *[Stephen J. Binz*, Advent of the Savior *(Liturgical Press, 1996) p. 15]*

We would be wise to recall that Jesus' family tree is our own: as the adopted children of the Father, we share the same ancestry, at once glorious and scandalous. And even now, Jesus is making Church out of *us*—the same kind of collection of sinners and saints and ordinary folks that make up any congregation. Bear that in mind when you look around at Midnight Mass and see unfamiliar faces, or the ones you see in church only at Christmas and Easter. Jesus was not ashamed to be born into a family with the same kind of faces.

Fougasse

⅓ cup warm water (100 to 110°)

1 pkg. active dry yeast

1 cup warm milk (100 to 110°)

½ cup (1 stick) butter, melted

1 tsp. salt

½ cup whole wheat flour

1 cup coarsely chopped walnuts

½ cup finely chopped onion

3 to 3 ½ cups unbleached all-
    purpose flour

Dissolve yeast in the warm water with a pinch of sugar—let stand until foamy, about 10 minutes. Combine yeast, milk, and whole wheat flour in a medium-size bowl and stir until blended.

Add butter, salt, walnuts, and onion and stir to combine. Add 3 cups unbleached flour, one cup at a time, mixing thoroughly after each addition to form a soft dough. Turn out onto a lightly floured board and knead for 5 or 6 minutes, adding small amounts of the remaining flour as needed to keep the dough manageable.

Place dough in a clean, greased bowl, and cover with a dry towel. Let rise in a warm place until doubled, about 1 hour. Punch down and knead a few strokes. On a lightly floured surface, roll dough into an oval about ½ inch thick. Place on a lightly greased baking sheet. Using a sharp knife or pizza cutter, make three or four pairs of diagonal cuts in the dough, as illustrated. Stretch dough apart to widen the cuts. Cover with a clean towel and let rise 30 to 45 minutes until nearly doubled.

Bake in a preheated 400° oven for 25 to 30 minutes, or until bread sounds hollow when tapped. Remove from baking sheet and cool on a wire rack.

Chapter Six

"She Wrapped Him in Swaddling Clothes and Laid Him in a Manger"

This verse from the gospel of the Mass at dawn on Christmas is so familiar to us that we can overlook its significance. Yet these simple phrases contain a wealth of symbolism and theological depth about Jesus' humanity, his ancestry, and his destiny. There are two breads that commemorate the Christ Child in his swaddling clothes, one of them quite ancient in origin, the other one relatively recent. Both are Saint Bede Abbey favorites.

The traditional Christmas bread that commemorates our Christmas passage is a German bread called stollen. It has a unique folded-over shape that is meant to symbolize the swaddling clothes. A friend of mine told me that her German mother instructed her to whisper her hopes and dreams into the dough and "fold them up tight" for the Christ Child to fulfill. Fr. Arthur's mother made it yearly for her family, and I have a photocopy of her recipe from the 1930s. There is also a "shortcut" version of stollen that is made much like shortcake or biscuit dough and requires about a quarter of the time. Both recipes are provided in this chapter.

A more recent Christmas baking tradition at Saint Bede is what I call Bambino Bread. Just about any yeast bread dough may be used to make it, since it's the shaping of the bread that makes it special. The dough is rolled out into a long rope and then twisted in a knot or braid that looks just like a baby wrapped in swaddling clothes. Follow the simple diagrams, and you can have a sweet bambino to grace your holiday table.

Clearly, the idea of swaddling clothes has captured the Christian imagination over the centuries. There is only one other reference to swaddling clothes in the Scriptures, in reference to one of Jesus' ancestors, Solomon:

> And I too, when born, inhaled the common air,
>> and fell upon the kindred earth;
>> wailing, I uttered that first sound common to all.
> In swaddling clothes and with constant care I was nurtured.
> For no king has any different origin or birth,
>> but one is the entry into life for all; and in one same way
>> they leave it.

(Wisdom 7:3-6.)

This text suggests that swaddling clothes are symbolic of common humanity, that even kings and messiahs enter the world like other human beings. Thus, Luke's mention of swaddling clothes is a way of affirming that Jesus is fully human, of the house and lineage of David, and therefore the heir to all the Davidic promises: "Your house and your kingdom shall endure forever before me; your throne shall stand firm forever" (2Samuel 7:16).

The mention of the manger in Luke's birth narrative is no less significant. After all, the text never specifies that Jesus was born in a stable, but we infer that from the mention of a manger, that is, a container for animal feed. The text goes on to explain: "There was no room for them in the inn" (Luke 2:7). This simple phrase sums up what must have been an agony of frustration and anxiety for Joseph and Mary as they pushed through the crowded streets of Bethlehem. They have arrived with nothing but a few meager supplies for the journey, and once arrived they have nowhere to go.

Scripture scholar Eugene Laverdiere notes that the word for "inn" in Greek means "place to put down your packs," suggesting that there isn't even a shade tree or public bench to provide a respite, let alone a room. In fact, many scholars suggest that even our Christmas card image of a spacious stable is too much. The text only says that Mary laid her child "in a manger," which could mean a feedbox in the open-air courtyard of a caravansary, perhaps with only a cloth awning overhead. In the midst of our celebrations we would do well to recall that in such poverty was the Savior presented to the world. The shapes of Christmas stollen and bambino bread can help remind us of holy simplicity, and of our Christian obligation to solidarity with and special care for the poor.

Traditional German Stollen

2 pkg. active dry yeast

2 cups lukewarm milk
   (100 to 110°)

1 pound of butter, softened

1 cup sugar

4 whole eggs

grated rind of 1 large lemon
   or orange

8 to 10 cups of all-purpose flour,
   divided

1 cup candied cherries

1 ½ cups dried mixed fruit

1 ½ cups chopped almonds
   melted butter

In a small bowl, dissolve yeast in warm milk and stir in one cup of flour; set aside to allow yeast to develop. In a large mixing bowl, cream the butter with the sugar until fluffy. Add the eggs, one at a time, and beat well. Add the yeast mixture and the lemon rind and stir until blended.

Add the flour, one cup at a time, until you have a soft dough that pulls away from the sides of the bowl. Turn out onto a lightly floured surface and knead until smooth and elastic, adding small amounts of flour to keep the dough manageable. Do not over knead—the dough should be soft rather than stiff. Cover and let rise until double in bulk, about 60 to 90 minutes. In a separate bowl, toss the fruits and nuts with a little flour to keep them from sticking together.

Punch dough down and knead briefly to expel large air bubbles. Flatten the dough and sprinkle the fruits and nuts on top. Fold in the corners and knead until fruit and nuts are evenly distributed in the dough. Divide dough into 3 or more portions. Roll each portion out into an oblong about 1 inch thick. Spread the top with melted butter, press down the center of the dough with the edge of your hand, and fold dough over double into a long loaf. Place on a greased baking sheet. Brush melted butter over the top and let rise until doubled, 30 to 45 minutes.

Bake at 350° for 35 to 45 minutes. Cover tops of loaves loosely with foil if they begin to brown too quickly. Remove from oven and cool on wire racks. While still slightly warm, drizzle on icing and sprinkle with chopped nuts or more fruit. Makes three large loaves.

Most stollen recipes are yeasted breads that take several hours to prepare. This one can be finished in just over an hour.

Preheat oven to 375°. Cream together butter and sugar until light and fluffy. Add the egg, sour cream, and lemon rind and beat thoroughly.

In a separate bowl, combine flour, baking powder, baking soda, and salt; stir until well blended. Gradually add flour mixture to liquids and stir until thoroughly blended. Fold in raisins and nuts until evenly distributed.

Lightly grease a 10 × 14 inch cookie sheet or jelly roll pan. Using buttered hands, shape the dough into a large oval. Brush the top of the dough with more butter, then fold half the dough not quite all the way over the other half.

Place immediately in the oven and bake for 40 to 45 minutes, or until lightly browned and a toothpick inserted in the center of the loaf comes out clean. Remove loaf to a wire rack to cool for several minutes, then brush the top with more butter. Serve warm or cool, sprinkled with powdered sugar.

Note: Do not substitute margarine, especially not for the butter brushed on top. Margarine has more salt and it will ruin both the taste and the texture of the bread.

Biscuit Stollen

½ cup butter

½ cup sugar

1 cup sour cream

1 egg

1 Tbs. freshly grated lemon rind

3 cups all-purpose flour

2 tsp. baking powder

1 tsp. baking soda

½ tsp. salt

1 cup raisins

1 cup slivered almonds

softened butter for shaping

powdered sugar for topping

Bambino
Bread

Use any recipe that will make a single loaf of bread, and allow the dough to rise once. The recipe for Buttermilk Sweet Dough on page 9 will be suitable. Punch down and knead dough briefly to work out the larger air bubbles. Roll the dough into a rope about 24 inches long, and form the braid as illustrated. Place on a lightly greased baking sheet; cover with a clean, dry towel and let rise for 30 minutes or until doubled. Bake in a preheated 350° oven for 25 to 30 minutes.

1.

2.

3.

Chapter Seven

"Watching Their Flocks by Night"

We have an image of the shepherds that comes from Christmas cards. All of them are roughly dressed but clean, well-groomed, and reverent. There's usually a boy with a flute, serenading the flock, and an old man carrying a lamb. They look like medieval versions of honest American livestock farmers, the kind you'd like to have as your neighbor down the road.

In fact, shepherds in first-century Palestine were the lowest rung on the ladder of agricultural workers. Most of them worked for wealthy men who didn't care to sleep out in the open with a herd of smelly animals. Shepherds were considered lazy, thieving ruffians who could barely be trusted with protecting the flock. These social and economic outcasts were the ones to whom God sent an angel with the news of the Savior's birth, accompanied by the heavenly host singing, "Gloria in excelsis Deo!"

Let's face it, most of us would not have been the recipients of that glorious message. It's the people on the margins of society who catch on to things in the Christmas story. Herod, the priests and scribes, the people of

Jerusalem all receive the news—Herod tries to have the child killed, the scribes quote the Scriptures but don't travel to Bethlehem to see them fulfilled, the people of Jerusalem go about their business.

Who then receives the Good News and responds? A young girl, pregnant but unmarried. An uneducated carpenter. An elderly couple and their unborn son. Ignorant shepherds and weird foreigners following a star. The gospels remind us in this season that piles of presents around the tree do not guarantee a Christmas well-celebrated. Perhaps one way to regain some simplicity is to make Basque Sheepherders' Bread.

Shepherds have been making large breads in pots for centuries. They mix the dough the night before and let it rise slowly in cool night air, then they bury the kettle in the ashes of their fire. When they return in the evening, the bread is finished. The first hunk of bread torn off the loaf is traditionally given to the sheepherder's dog, as an acknowledgment of its essential role in the labor of keeping the flock together and in good health. Make one in honor of the shepherds in the Christmas story and share it with the hard working people in your life. A large loaf of homemade bread accompanied by a tub of butter and a jar of preserves is a welcome addition to any breakroom.

Basque Sheepherders' Bread

In a large mixing bowl, combine hot water, butter, sugar, and salt. Stir until butter melts and let cool to lukewarm. Stir in yeast until dissolved, then cover to let yeast develop, about 10 minutes.

Add 5 cups flour and beat with heavy-duty mixer or wooden spoon to form a thick batter. Stir in enough of the remaining flour to form a stiff dough. Turn out onto a lightly floured board and knead until the dough is smooth and elastic, about 10 to 12 minutes. Place dough back in the rinsed bowl and lightly grease the surface. Cover and let rise in a warm place until doubled, about 1 ½ hours.

Punch down dough and knead for 2 minutes, then form into a smooth ball. Cut a circle of foil to cover bottom of a Dutch oven. Grease insides of Dutch oven and underside of lid with shortening, salad oil, or cooking spray. Place the ball of dough in the pot and cover with lid. Let dough rise in a warm place until the dough just starts to push up the lid—this takes about 45 minutes to an hour, but watch closely.

Bake covered with the lid in a preheated 375° oven for 12 minutes. Remove lid and bake 30 to 35 minutes more or until loaf is golden brown and sounds hollow. Remove from oven and allow to cool for about 15 minutes before turning loaf out onto a cooling rack—you may need a helper for this.

3 cups hot water

½ cup butter (1 stick)

½ cup sugar

2 ½ tsp. salt

2 pkg. active dry yeast

9 ½ cups flour; approximately
(bread flour is best, but up to
4 cups could be whole wheat)

Detail of Window, Saint Mary's Church, Peru, Illinois

Chapter Eight

"A Multitude of the Heavenly Host"

There isn't a traditional bread in honor of the angels, so I decided to invent one. Both my birth family and my monastic family love homemade dinner rolls, so I came up with "Herbal Angel Horns." You can have these easy rolls mixed up, shaped, and rising in less than 25 minutes. They rise for an hour, during which time you can be finishing other meal preparations, then they bake for a speedy 12 to 15 minutes. So in just over half an hour of actual work, you can have fresh rolls on the table for Christmas dinner. They're made much like crescent rolls, but instead of rolling up from the bottom edge, these are rolled from the side to form a trumpet.

The herbs used are parsley and marjoram. Parsley symbolizes hospitality and feasting, and so represents our welcoming the Christ Child as well as welcoming our families to holiday meals. Marjoram symbolizes joy because of the exuberant way it blooms, and it reminds us of the angel's message: "Behold, I proclaim to you good news of great joy" (Luke 2:10).

Herbal Angel Horns

1 cup milk

3 ¼ cups all-purpose flour, divided

2 Tbs. butter

1 Tbs. dried parsley

2 Tbs. sugar

2 tsp. dried marjoram

1 large egg, beaten

1 tsp. salt

1 pkg. fast-rising dry yeast

Mix yeast with 2 cups flour, parsley, marjoram, and salt in a medium-size bowl; set aside. Combine milk, butter, and sugar in a small saucepan over medium heat—scald but do not allow to boil. Cool mixture to 130°. Stir milk mixture into flour mixture along with the egg and beat until thoroughly combined.

Stir in another cup of flour (the remaining quarter cup of flour is reserved for kneading) and mix thoroughly. Knead for about three minutes, dusting the dough with small amounts of the remaining flour. Cover with a clean, dry towel and let rest for 5 minutes.

Divide dough in half. Roll each half into a circle roughly 12 inches in diameter. With a sharp knife or pizza cutter, divide dough into 8 wedges. Brush the top of each wedge *lightly* with water—just enough to make it sticky. Starting with one of the long sides of the triangle, roll up into a trumpet shape. Place rolls seam side down on a lightly greased cookie sheet. Repeat with remaining dough (use two cookie sheets to avoid crowding). Allow to rise, covered, in a warm place free from drafts for about 60 minutes or until doubled.

Bake in a preheated 350° oven for 12 to 15 minutes or until golden brown. Makes 16 rolls.

When I was growing up, my mother regularly made crescent rolls. We referred to them as "Fred Flintstone Telephone Rolls," because to us children they looked like the telephones on the cartoon. When they were served, it was the one time we were allowed to play with our food: we could pretend to call someone else at the table on our "roll phones." So if you serve these Angel Horns and the little ones at the table play with their food by pretending to blow the angel's trumpets, just let them—it's Christmas!

Although I said before that there aren't any traditional angel breads, I learned from my Polish friend Chet Tomczak there is a traditional Polish treat made at Christmas called "kruschiki" or "little wings." These rich little cookies are made with sour cream and egg yolks (and sometimes a little whisky or rum!), fried in oil and coated with powdered sugar. Like most fried foods they are best served immediately after making them, but the recipe is simple and dough can be refrigerated before use, so with a little advance planning you can have them fresh for dessert. They are also a delicious addition to a Christmas tea party.

Kruschiki

→ pull through

Mix flour and sugar in a small bowl and stir to combine thoroughly. In another small bowl, beat eggs with the sour cream (and the liquor if desired) and stir to form a soft dough. Wrap the dough in plastic wrap and refrigerate for at least an hour (it may be refrigerated overnight).

Take half the dough and place it on a lightly floured board. Dust the surface of the dough with a little flour to keep the rolling pin from sticking, and roll out to a rectangle about 10 × 12 inches. (Make sure that the dough isn't sticking to the counter before you cut—sprinkle additional flour under the dough as needed). Using a pizza cutter or sharp knife, cut dough into 1 ½-inch strips. Then cut strips on the diagonal to form diamonds about 4 inches tall. Make a 1-inch horizontal slit in the center of each strip, then pull one end of the strip through the slit to form the pair of wings (see illustration). Repeat with remaining dough. Fry the kruschiki a few at a time in oil heated to 375˚.

Fry about 1 minute per side or until golden brown. Drain the cookies on paper towels, then toss in powdered sugar. Serve warm.

1 ½ cups flour

2 Tbs. sugar

4 egg yolks

⅓ cup sour cream

1 or 2 Tbs. whisky or rum
   (optional)

vegetable oil for frying

powdered sugar for coating

Chapter Nine

"There Came Wise Men from the East"

Twelfth Night is the feast of the Epiphany, the Twelfth Day of Christmas in the old calendar. Although we associate "King Cake" with Mardis Gras, it was originally a sweet bread served on Epiphany in honor of the three kings. The bread should contain a dried bean, and whoever gets the bean is king or queen for the day and receives a small gift. I have included two recipes for Epiphany, one for a traditional yeasted bread from Portugal called Bolo-Rei, the other for a rich chocolate cake flavored with orange.

The story of the visit of the Magi to the newborn King is unique to Matthew's gospel, and it was celebrated with its own feast as early as the second half of the fourth century. Tradition has handed down their names as Caspar, Melchior, and Balthazar, but the gospel account is vague: it simple names them as Magi or "wise men." There has been considerable scholarly debate as to the Magi's number, origin, religion, and even their existence. Let's leave that discussion in more capable hands and see what we can learn from looking at the story as Matthew tells it. Three things in particular stand out to me as being significant for our own faith journey (I should note that some of these insights came from a talk given some years ago by my friend and colleague Dawn Williams):

The Magi made a long journey in the dark. The text specifies that the Magi were guided on their quest for the newborn King by a star. This journey in the night can be symbolic of our own pilgrimage of faith: on our journey to the kingdom, rarely do we travel in the full light of certitude, under a blazing sun of confidence and clarity. More often, it seems, we travel in the twilight of hope, where faith and fear blend gradually one into the other as sunset fades into night, with the gospel star shining on the horizon, guiding us to our encounter with the Word Made Flesh. But we have an advantage over those travelers of old: we already know the One for whom we seek.

They were willing to face danger and evil for the sake of the true king. Even under the relatively peaceful and stable rule of the Roman Empire (the famous *pax Romana*), travel was still difficult and dangerous. The risk of accident or injury was always present, and desert bandits were not uncommon. Further, Herod's reputation for violence could hardly have escaped the Magi's notice. Yet they faced the dangers of travel and risked an encounter with an evil ruler because they were so driven by their desire to meet Jesus. Often, our modern society is no less hostile to gospel values; how firm is *our* resolve?

They went home by another way. One can easily miss this short sentence at the end of the gospel, or dismiss it as a minor detail. In all honesty, it probably held no great importance in the mind of the evangelist. But I think it holds the key to our whole celebration of Christmas. We spend all of Advent preparing to meet the Promised One. At Christmas we hear the familiar stories of Elizabeth and Zechariah, Mary and Joseph, Jesus in his swaddling clothes, shepherds in the field, and angels in the heavens. Like the Magi, we kneel before the crib, we offer our gifts at the altar, we encounter the Savior, newborn in our hearts. And if we are wise, we will also go home by another way. Our Christmas experiences should *change us*, so that our encounter with Christ in the season, in the Word proclaimed, in the sacrament of the bread made flesh, will not allow us to go back to the same old ways of living, the same old patterns of speaking and choosing and acting. Rather, we must choose a new path, set out on a new journey, renewed in faith and hope, guided not by a star but by the Spirit speaking within us.

Bolo-Rei

1 pkg. active dry yeast

¾ cup lukewarm milk

⅓ cup sugar

¼ cup (½ stick) butter, melted

2 eggs, room temperature

½ tsp. salt

3 ½ cups all-purpose flour,
    divided

½ cup candied orange peel

¼ cup candied lemon peel

½ cup sliced almonds

a large dried bean

½ cup apricot preserves

2 Tbs. orange juice

10 to 12 glazed red cherry halves

extra sliced almonds for topping

Sprinkle yeast in the warm milk with a pinch of the sugar; stir to dissolve and let stand until foamy. Add sugar, melted butter, eggs, and salt and stir until thoroughly mixed. Add 3 cups of the flour, one cup at a time, stirring after each addition until flour is thoroughly incorporated.

Turn the dough out onto a lightly floured board and knead for 6 minutes, using small amounts of the remaining flour to keep the dough manageable. The dough will be quite soft and rather sticky, but resist adding too much flour or the bread will be dry. Flatten the dough into an oval, place the candied fruit and nuts on top, roll up into a ball and knead until the fruit and nuts are evenly distributed.

Place the dough into the rinsed bowl and cover with a clean, dry towel. Let rise until doubled in bulk, about 60 to 90 minutes. Punch dough down and knead briefly to expel the large air bubbles. Insert the bean into the dough and shape the dough into a ring. Place the ring on a lightly greased baking sheet and cover with a clean, dry towel. Let rise again until nearly doubled, 30 to 45 minutes.

While the bread is rising, preheat oven to 350°. Bake ring for 30 minutes, or until golden brown and the loaf sounds hollow when tapped on the bottom. Remove from pan and cool on a wire rack.

Just before serving, make the glaze by combining the apricot preserves and orange juice in a small saucepan and warming over low heat until liquid. Brush the top and the sides of the ring with the glaze, decorate with cherries and sliced almonds, and serve.

Orange Chocolate King Cake

If you're short on time and can't make the yeasted bread in the Bolo-Rei, try this rich cake instead.

Preheat oven to 350°. Cream together butter and sugar until light and fluffy. Beat in eggs, sour cream, zest, juice, and almond extract. In a separate bowl, sift together flour, baking powder, baking soda, and salt. Add gradually to the sugar mixture until well blended. Fold in chocolate chips and almonds.

Spoon batter into a greased and floured Bundt pan. Bake for 1 hour and 15 minutes, or until a cake tester inserted in the center of the cake comes out clean. Let cool for about 10 minutes before removing cake from pan. May be served as is or with a light glaze.

1 cup (2 sticks) butter, softened

1 cup sugar

3 large eggs

2 cups sour cream

zest and juice of two medium oranges

1 Tbs. almond extract

3 cups all-purpose flour

1 Tbs. baking powder

2 tsp. baking soda

½ tsp. salt

1 ½ cups semi-sweet chocolate chips

1 ½ cups sliced almonds

Detail of Window, Saint John the Baptist Church, Bradford, Illinois

Chapter Ten

"We Have Seen His Star"

Because the wise men were guided by a star, stars are a common element of Christmas decorations and foods (think of the top of a Christmas tree and cut-out sugar cookies, for example). So it's not surprising that there is a Christmas bread that is star-shaped. Although pannetone is the traditional Christmas bread in Italy, pan d'oro (golden bread) is gaining in popularity, and it was recommended to me by native Italians as well as fellow monks who studied in Rome. Pan d'oro is traditionally made in a tall, star-shaped pan, available at many specialty shops and online. It can also be made in regular loaf pans, brioche pans, or a Bundt cake pan. But a golden star-shaped loaf dusted with powdered sugar makes a dramatic addition to the Christmas buffet or dinner table, so it's worth the effort to get one of the traditional pans.

Stars are found in other biblical passages as well. A striking example is found in Numbers 24:17, in which a seer named Balaam proclaims an oracle about the people of Israel who are entering Palestine to take possession of the land:

> I see him, though not now;
>> I behold him, though not near:
> A star shall advance from Jacob,
>> and a staff shall arise from Israel.

It is likely this oracle is meant to refer to the Israelites themselves as personified by their ancestor Jacob, or it may be meant to represent the coming Davidic dynasty. Many of the early church writers saw this as a prophecy about the coming Messiah, a prophecy fulfilled by Jesus, who is viewed as both the star and the staff—both guiding light and daily support for the people of God.

The peoples of the ancient world believed that the appearance of a new star or comet was supposed to herald the birth of important rulers. For example, one was supposed to have accompanied the birth of Alexander the Great. Just what was the star that heralded the birth of Jesus? If it appeared suddenly, there would be a record of it in other ancient writings, since many cultures in the ancient world had developed the science of astronomy to a remarkably sophisticated level.

It could have been a nova or supernova, although no other historical record mentions one, or it could have been a comet (one appeared in 5 BC). Most likely it was the conjunction of the planets Jupiter and Saturn, a rare astronomical event. It happened four times in 7 BC: May 27, September 15 (also in alignment with the earth and the sun, which rarely happens), October 6, and December 1. An additional clue comes from the fact that the conjunction took place in the section of the sky ruled by the constellation Pisces, which ancient astronomers viewed as symbolic of the Jewish people. Thus, the Magi knew to search the land of Judah for the newborn King.

Paradoxically, the glorious star that lighted their way guided them to a humble place: an ordinary house in a small Judean town. In spite of what we normally see in nativity scenes and Christmas cards, the travelers did not visit the Holy Family while they were in the stable. By the time the Magi arrived, the census was long over and it would have no longer been necessary to be living there. In fact, the gospel specifies: "on entering the *house* they saw the child with Mary his mother" (Matthew 2:11, emphasis added). But this borrowed or rented dwelling could hardly have been luxurious. Most likely it had a single room that served as dining room, living room, and sleeping quarters, perhaps with no opening for light except the narrow doorway.

If we would be wise this Christmas, we should let the Christmas star guide us not to luxury and excess, but to the simple and humble place where Love dwells. Let us enter by the narrow door, stooping to cross the threshold of humility, and kneeling to offer our gift: the priceless treasure of our lives, ourselves.

Pan d'oro

In a medium-size bowl,
cream together butter and sugar. Add eggs and beat well. Add proofed yeast, milk, salt, and lemon extract if desired. Add flour and beat for 200 strokes. Cover batter and let rise for 60 to 75 minutes. Stir down, pour into a greased star-shaped pan d'oro pan (it should fill the pan about halfway). Allow to rise again for 20 to 30 minutes, or until batter reaches within 1 inch of the top of the pan.

1 pkg. yeast, proofed in ¼ cup
   of warm water

3 ½ cups all-purpose flour

1 ¼ cups sugar

¼ cup butter, softened

¾ cup whole milk

4 eggs

½ tsp. salt

1 ½ tsp. lemon extract
   (optional)

Bake in a preheated oven at
400° for 45 minutes, or until a cake tester comes out clean. Set pan on a cooling rack and allow loaf to cool for at least an hour before removing from pan. There may be a slight bulge on the bottom of the loaf—trim this off as needed to make a flat bottom. Sprinkle with powdered sugar.

Chapter Eleven

"They Offered Him Gifts of Gold, Frankincense, and Myrrh"

I don't have a recipe to represent the gifts of the Magi. Frankincense and myrrh are aromatic resins more noted for potpourri than for baking, and gold bread pans would be a bit too pricey for most of us. But these treasures offered to the newborn King have much to tell us about how to go about our own gift-giving.

The Magi's gifts were not only rich in value but also in symbolism. Gold was a sign of Jesus' kingship as the Son of David. Frankincense, which was used in worship services since ancient times, symbolized his divinity as the Son of God. Myrrh was one of the ointments used when preparing a body for burial, and therefore indicates Jesus' salvific death.

In some countries, such as Italy and Spain, children receive gifts on the feast of the Epiphany, in imitation of the Magi giving their gifts to the infant Jesus. No matter when we keep the custom of Christmas gift-giving, there is always a danger of excess. In a recent editorial in *Newsweek*, one journalist said that on

Christmas morning "it looked like a mall had thrown up in our living room."

We would do well to heed the example of the wise men in this matter and exercise some common sense and restraint. In the November 14, 2006, issue of *Woman's Day Magazine*, an article advised that we take a cue from the Magi's gifts of **G**old, **F**rankincense, and **M**yrrh, and offer our children only three gifts: a **G**arment, a **F**un gift, and something that is **M**entally stimulating, like a book or a puzzle. If our children are used to receiving far more, an explanation early in the season would be advisable, perhaps as a topic of discussion when the family is together for Thanksgiving.

Another aspect of holiday gift-giving is suggested by a little-known book written by Henry Van Dyke (1852–1933), an American author and clergyman who taught English literature at Princeton. He wrote a number of Christmas stories, and in 1895 he published *The Story of the Other Wise Man*. In it, he traces the journey of Artaban, a Persian astronomer who is a colleague of Caspar, Melchior, and Balthazar and intends to join them on their journey. He sells his possessions to purchase three great jewels—a sapphire, a ruby, and a pearl—to give as his gift to the newborn King. He then travels to meet his companions outside the walls of Babylon.

Artaban never meets with his fellow Magi, nor does he ever reach his goal of paying homage to the King. He is unable to join his companions' caravan because he stops to care for a dangerously ill Hebrew exile, who directs him to Bethlehem. He is forced to sell his sapphire to assemble his own caravan. At Bethlehem he discovers that the Holy Family has already fled, and he uses the ruby as a bribe to keep the captain of Herod's soldiers from taking the child of a woman who has offered him hospitality.

For thirty-three years Artaban travels all over the East in search of the elusive King, all the while continuing to heal the sick, feed the hungry, and comfort the afflicted. Finally, he comes at last to Jerusalem, just as "the King of the Jews" is being led to Golgotha. But before he can use the pearl to ransom Jesus from his enemies, he encounters a Persian girl who is being sold into slavery for her father's debts. He gives the pearl to ransom her from her captives.

Later, as Artaban lies dying, he hears the voice of Jesus commending him for his care for "the least of these my brethren":

> A calm radiance of wonder and joy lighted the pale face of Artaban like the first ray of dawn on a snowy mountain-peak. One long, last breath of relief exhaled gently from his lips.
>
> His journey was ended. His treasures were accepted. The other Wise Man had found the King.

This lovely story was republished in 1984 by Random House and is still in print, and a film version was made in 1985 starring Martin Sheen, which is also still available.

The story of the fourth wise man, although not biblical, offers some inspiration for holiday gift-giving. We can remind our children—and ourselves—that it is Jesus' birthday, not ours, and we should first think of what gifts we might offer him before shopping for each other. Like Artaban, we can lay gifts at the feet of Jesus by our care for the least of his brothers and sisters. Here are some suggestions:

- On the first Sunday of Advent, read Matthew 25: 31-46 aloud, and discuss ways that the family can fulfill each of the traditional "Corporal Works of Mercy": feed the hungry, give drink to the thirsty, clothe the naked, shelter the homeless, care for the sick, visit the imprisoned, and bury the dead. Try to do more than write a check (although that's a good start) by getting personally involved in Christian action for each of these areas.
- Have family members nominate causes for which they would like to send a sizable donation, and determine what the family can give up or sacrifice in order to make that donation. You might bake Bolo-Rei with its hidden bean, and the person who gets the bean is designated as Artaban, who then must be the wise person to choose which charity to support.
- Be especially mindful of those who have lost a loved one in the past year. The first Christmas without them is likely to be difficult. A simple

note or brief phone call expressing your concern for them can make a big difference. You're not expected to play therapist—you don't have to write much or talk long (unless you sense they have a need to share their feelings).

We would be truly wise if we heed the wisdom of the readings of Advent. Many of them emphasize not Jesus' first coming as a baby, but his second coming as Savior and judge. By viewing Christmas in the context of preparing for that day when "the Son of Man comes in his glory, and all the angels with him," we can more easily resist the tendency to focus too much upon the things of this world. Mindful that "he will sit upon his glorious throne, and all the nations will be assembled before him" for judgment, we can make conscious choices about our holiday spending, rather than blindly accepting our society's materialistic values. Above all, we can celebrate Christmas in such a fashion as to deserve to hear our Savior say to us: "Amen, I say to you, whatever you did for one of these least brothers of mine, you did for me" (cf Mt 25:31-46).

Here I am with Zachary, one of the nephews mentioned in the following pages. This was taken at his First Holy Communion, one of the many occasions for which the family gets together for food and fellowship throughout the year.

Chapter Twelve

A Family Christmas Brunch

Since I joined the monastery, my family has kept the tradition of celebrating Christmas together on or near the Sunday after Christmas, on the feast of the Holy Family. For centuries, Christians celebrated the birth of Jesus from December 25 to January 6; that is, from the Nativity to the feast of Epiphany, the traditional "Twelve Days of Christmas" (and you probably thought that was just a counting carol!). Celebrating in this way has a number of advantages.

First, it's less rushed. Rather than trying to gather with one's immediate family, extended family, in-laws, etc., all within a 36-hour period, you have time to enjoy several celebrations over a number of days, with a few breaks in between. Anyone who has rushed from house to house on Christmas Day with children, presents, and potluck in tow can see the wisdom in this custom. You can have Christmas Eve with grandparents, a relaxed

Christmas morning with your family in their pajamas, and a day with your siblings later in the week. You can enjoy Christmas religious services without checking your watch and worrying about traffic. While there is something to be said for huge family celebrations at Grandma's, they can also be so exhausting as to defeat the purpose of the season—especially for Grandma!

Secondly, multiple celebrations mean that you have more down time to recover, regroup, and re-energize. There's no need to have every single gift wrapped (or even purchased!) by Christmas Eve, nor do you have to prepare everyone's favorite holiday foods in a single afternoon. One celebration can be a formal meal with everyone dressed up, another might be a simple buffet, another could be nothing more complex than cookies and hot chocolate with gift-giving mixed in. You might choose one special holiday food or simple activity to do as a family each day between Christmas and Epiphany, rather than trying to do it all between Midnight Mass and Christmas night.

The real advantage to this kind of extended holiday season is that it eases the pressure to have everything perfect with only one chance to get it right. We have these nostalgic images of the perfect Christmas, either from our childhood or from popular culture, and we can feel our Christmas has to live up to that impossibly high standard. By spreading the cheer (and therefore, the preparations) over twelve days, there is less emphasis on having a single "perfect" event.

As I suggested before, my family Christmas celebration at the abbey is certainly less than picture perfect. After all, it's held in our Academy's student dining room, with few if any decorations (although everyone sneaks into the monastery refectory to take family pictures in front of the huge abbey Christmas tree!). We use ordinary paper plates and plastic cups, none of the serving dishes match, and usually we use the cafeteria stainless steel hot cart to keep the food warm. Let's face it, *Better Homes and Gardens* magazine is not going to be featuring this venue anytime soon. But we have plenty of room and an abundance of good cheer, and that's what counts.

There is also an abundance of good, simple food. Although pizza is the perennial favorite, some years we have a Christmas brunch. The recipes that follow are some of our favorites, some adapted from my previous cookbooks, others being published for the first time here. Mind you, I have never made all of these at once in a single year! But you may find one or two that will become your favorites as well.

Buffet-style Scrambled Eggs

This is a recipe I'm serving at Christmas brunch for the first time this year. I'm sure I'll have to serve regular scrambled eggs as well, since some of my nephews are particular about their breakfast! But I think some of my sibs are going to like these a lot—a couple of my stage crew kids certainly did when I tested the recipe with them. If your grocery store carries fresh herbs year-round, it's worth the effort and expense to get them for these eggs.

2 Tbs. butter

2 Tbs. all-purpose flour

1 cup milk

2 tsp. instant chicken bouillon

8 eggs

Fresh parsley, thyme, and/or chives (optional)

Melt butter in a small saucepan over medium heat; stir in flour until smooth. Add the milk and bouillon, then whisk smooth. Turn heat up to medium high and bring to a boil until thickened (about 2 minutes), whisking constantly. Remove from heat and set aside.

Beat eggs and cook in a nonstick pan over medium heat, stirring occasionally, until they are nearly but not quite set. Add the sauce and stir gently, cooking until the eggs are completely set. Salt and pepper to taste. Garnish with fresh minced herbs before serving if desired.

I developed these individual serving casseroles, so you can make as few or as many as you like. I served these for my family Christmas a few years ago, and they were a huge hit. Fortunately, we have a number of ovenproof soup bowls with handles that are just the perfect serving size. I actually prepared these casseroles the night before, covered them with plastic wrap, and refrigerated them until I was ready to put them in the oven. I had to increase the baking time to about 45 minutes, but they were perfect.

French Toast Custard Casseroles

Preheat oven to 350°. Lightly coat the interior of the ovenproof bowl with cooking spray or butter. Trim bread slices to a shape and size that will fit the bowl. In another larger bowl, whisk egg and milk, then place bread slices in egg mixture until liquid is absorbed.

Combine nuts and syrup in the bottom of the ovenproof bowl, and dot the surface with the butter. Place the soaked bread slices on top—they should not reach past the lip of the bowl.

Place bowl on a baking sheet to prevent drips, and place in the preheated oven. Bake for 30 to 35 minutes, until top is lightly browned and center is firm. Remove from oven and allow to set for about 10 minutes. Invert bowl onto a plate, remove bowl and serve.

For each casserole, you will need:

1 egg

2 Tbs. whole or reduced-fat milk

2 thick or 3 medium slices of day-old bread

2 Tbs. chopped pecans

⅓ cup maple-flavored syrup

1 Tbs. butter

1 ovenproof bowl, about 5 inches across and 2 inches deep

(From *More Breaking Bread with Father Dominic*, 2001)

Apricot Skillet Bread

1 cup yogurt (plain or flavored)

2 tsp. baking powder

2 cups chopped apricots

2 cups yellow cornmeal

2 eggs (or egg substitute)

1 cup spelt flour (or all-purpose)

1 Tbs. wheat germ

2 Tbs. brown sugar

2 tsp. ground ginger

1 tsp. ground coriander seed

2 tsp. salt

This bread is for the health-conscious at your Christmas party. The flavors of this bread are quite subtle, so try it warm by itself before adding toppings. We discovered that a light hand with the butter knife and just a small drizzle of honey accented the taste without overwhelming it. Spelt, by the way, is a grain cultivated since antiquity, and it is more easily digested than wheat flours. I like the slightly sweet, nutty character it adds to bread. Spelt flour may not be readily available in your area, so feel free to substitute all-purpose flour.

Apricot Skillet Bread

(continued)

Preheat oven to 400°. In a medium-size saucepan, warm yogurt over low heat until liquid. Remove from heat and add apricots and eggs; stir until blended.

In another bowl, mix all dry ingredients thoroughly. Lightly grease a 10-inch cast-iron skillet and place in the oven for 5 minutes. Pour yogurt mixture onto dry ingredients and stir until just moistened.

Remove skillet from oven and pour in batter, smoothing the top with a spatula or spoon. Immediately place in oven and bake for at least 20 minutes. To test for doneness, insert a toothpick in the center of the bread and remove—if it comes out clean, the bread is done. If not, return to oven for 5 more minutes.

Leave in the pan for 5 minutes after it comes out of the oven. Then, remove the flatbread by placing one hand (protected by an oven mitt or towel) on top of the bread and turning the pan upside down with the other hand, catching the bread in your hand as it comes out. If bread does not come out easily, allow to cool in pan for a few more minutes, then try again. Allow to cool on a wire rack for 10 more minutes, then cut into wedges and serve.

(From *Breaking Bread with Father Dominic*, 1999)

Cornmeal Bacon Pancakes with Honey Sauce

1 ½ cups yellow cornmeal

1 tsp. salt

1 ½ cups boiling water

2 Tbs. butter

1 cup flour

1 Tbs. baking powder

2 eggs

2 Tbs. molasses

1 cup milk

1 cup cooked chopped bacon

I love cornmeal bread with honey, so these pancakes are among my favorite recipes. The combination of the slightly crunchy texture of cornmeal with the salty bacon and the sweet sauce is irresistible. The sauce, incidentally, isn't as sweet as plain maple syrup and doesn't leave you with that last-soggy-bite slight nausea. Stone-ground cornmeal is my preference for these flapjacks, because I like the crunch, but you can use regular cornmeal for a more cake-like texture as well. If you want to serve these on a buffet table and you don't have a large griddle, place a clean dish towel on a cookie sheet. As you complete pancakes place them on the towel in a single layer, cover with another towel and keep them warm in the oven. Make a second layer with another towel as necessary.

Place cornmeal, salt, and butter in a medium-size bowl and stir in boiling water until butter is melted and mixed in. Let stand while you assemble other ingredients.

Sift flour and baking powder together into a separate bowl and stir to combine thoroughly. Combine eggs, molasses, milk, and bacon; beat well. Add egg mixture to cornmeal and stir. Gently stir in flour and baking powder until just combined—do not over beat. Allow mixture to thicken while the griddle is heating.

Drop onto hot, lightly oiled griddle. When holes form on the top of the pancake that do not close, flip over and cook until lightly browned on the other side. Makes 12 to 16 pancakes.

Honey Sauce

Combine ingredients in a small saucepan and cook over low to medium heat. Stir until ingredients are completely combined and heated through. Use warm over pancakes—also excellent with Gingerbread Waffles (see page 67).

¼ cup (½ stick) of butter

1 ½ cups honey

¾ cup maple syrup

½ tsp. ground cinnamon
    (optional)

Eggnog Waffles

3 cups all-purpose flour

1 Tbs. baking powder

1 ½ tsp. baking soda

½ tsp. salt

3 eggs, beaten

3 cups eggnog

½ cup (1 stick) butter, melted

1 cup chopped pecans, toasted

1 cup chopped candied cherries

My young chef-in-training Kevin and I had a great time developing this recipe, and they were a huge hit at Christmas Brunch. This recipe is a great way to use up eggnog that's leftover from a holiday party, but it's worth buying the eggnog just for the waffles!

If you have some extra batter, make one or two waffles for the freezer. Just cook the waffles slightly drier than usual (otherwise they go mushy) and wait for them to cool completely before wrapping individual servings in plastic wrap. They keep in the freezer for about three months (not that they'll last that long!). Reheat in the toaster rather than the microwave—you'll be glad you did.

In a medium-size bowl, sift together baking powder, baking soda, and salt; stir to combine. In a separate bowl, combine eggs, eggnog, and butter and mix well. Add egg mixture to dry ingredients; mix until smooth but do not over beat. Fold in nuts and cherries.

Bake in preheated waffle iron until browned—follow manufacturer's instructions regarding time and temperature. Makes six.

This recipe uses the same spices as gingerbread, so it makes the house smell like Christmas. These spiced waffles can be served with many different toppings. Try them with the usual butter and syrup, or with a warm fruit compote (use canned pie filling in a pinch), or with a dollop of French vanilla ice cream. Here's a tip for whisking egg whites—using a cold bowl helps speed up the process, so if you know you're going to make waffles in the morning, put a small mixing bowl in the fridge the night before.

Gingerbread Waffles

¾ cup milk

¼ cup vegetable oil

¼ cup molasses

2 eggs, separated

1 ½ cups all-purpose flour

¼ cup sugar

1 ½ tsp. baking powder

½ tsp. baking soda

½ tsp. salt

½ tsp. cinnamon

½ tsp. ginger

¼ tsp. nutmeg

Sift dry ingredients into a medium-size bowl. In a separate bowl, mix milk, oil, molasses, and egg yolks, and stir into dry ingredients until just moistened. Whisk egg whites until soft peaks appear and gently fold them into the mixture.

Bake in preheated waffle iron until browned—follow manufacturer's instructions regarding time and temperature. Makes three large waffles.

(From *Breaking Bread with Father Dominic 2*)

Sausage Roll-ups

1 cup whole milk

1 large egg

½ cup + 2 Tbs. butter

1 pkg. yeast

¼ cup water

2 ½ to 2 ¾ cups of flour

1 tsp. salt

1 pound uncooked bulk
   breakfast sausage

My mother makes these nearly every year for Christmas brunch, and we devour them (although she will admit that she uses crescent roll dough in a tube!). For a breakfast buffet, serve them on a warming tray if you have one. You can also serve them as a hot appetizer by using a garlic or Italian sausage. Resist the temptation to turn them into mini-pizzas by adding sauce and cheese, because that would overpower the delicate texture of the pastry crust. If you're the kind of person who pours extra syrup on pancakes so there will be enough to dip your sausage into, try serving these with a tablespoon of maple syrup drizzled on top of each.

Sausage Roll-ups

(continued)

In a small bowl, proof yeast in the water. Warm milk and 2 Tbs. butter in a saucepan over medium heat until butter is melted. Stir in salt, then cool to lukewarm. Pour into large bowl and add yeast and egg. Add flour, ½ cup at a time.

Turn out onto lightly floured board and knead for about 2 minutes. Cover dough with a towel and allow to rest for about 5 minutes, so the dough will firm up. At this point you can refrigerate until the following morning, then remove from wrapping and allow to sit at room temperature for 15 minutes before proceeding.

Take a stick of softened butter (½ cup) and incorporate it into the dough by hand—you just squish it around until it can be kneaded. Knead 2 or 3 minutes on a lightly floured board, then let the dough rest for 5 minutes while you get out the sausage and lightly grease your baking sheets.

Roll the dough out into a rectangle—it should be very thin, a little less than ¼ inch thick. Spread a pound of uncooked breakfast sausage on top of the dough, then carefully roll it up like a jelly roll. Using a very sharp knife, cut thin slices, between ¼ inch to ½ inch thick.

Place slices on the baking sheet about 2 inches apart, and allow to rise, covered, for half an hour. Preheat oven to 350° and bake for 15 minutes, until sausage is browned and bread is golden brown.

(From *Breaking Bread with Father Dominic*, 1999)

Honey Oatmeal Bread

I get more requests for this recipe than any other, and if you want a special bread to go with any holiday meal, this is it. I include it here because it makes excellent toast. The dough for this bread will be somewhat stickier than other doughs, so be careful not to add too much flour. Doughs made with honey may darken more quickly than other breads. If the loaves start to get too dark in the oven, loosely cover them with aluminum foil and continue baking.

1 cup quick-cooking oats

⅓ cup honey

2 cups hot water

2 tsp. salt

1 pkg. dry yeast

1 Tbs. butter or oil

¼ cup warm water

5 cups of flour, approx.

Extra oatmeal for coating

1 egg (optional)

Put the oats in a large bowl. Bring 2 cups water to a boil, pour it over the oats and let stand for at least 15 minutes. Stir the yeast into ¼ cup of warm water and let stand for 5 minutes to dissolve. Feel the oats at the bottom of the bowl to be sure they're lukewarm, then add the honey, salt, butter, and dissolved yeast. You can also add an egg for an extra rich dough. Work in enough of the flour so that the dough can be handled, but remember that the oatmeal and the honey will make this a *very* sticky dough.

Turn out onto a lightly floured board, knead for a minute or two and then let rest for 10 minutes. Resume kneading until the dough is elastic, but still rather sticky—don't add too much flour at a time. Place in a greased bowl, cover, and let rise in a warm spot until double in bulk. Punch down and divide into two pieces. Knead each piece to remove the large air bubbles, but do not use any flour on the kneading board—you want the dough to remain sticky. Roll each loaf in the extra oatmeal until it is completely covered.

Place loaves on lightly greased cookie sheets and allow to rise until doubled. Preheat oven to 350°. Bake bread for 45 minutes. Remove from cookie sheets and cool on racks.

(From *Breaking Bread with Father Dominic*, 1999)

This is a variation on Victorian milk bread that I use whenever I want something simple but a little more special. The milk makes for a tender crumb and fine texture, and the egg, butter, and sugar make for a slightly richer, sweeter dough. It can be baked in loaf pans, formed into round or free-form loaves, braided, or used as a base for other recipes such as Rose Rolls, Bambino Bread, Povitica, and Ham and Cheese Braid.

Holiday Bread

2 cups lukewarm milk

2 pkg. active dry yeast

¼ cup sugar

1 beaten egg

¼ cup (½ stick) butter, melted

2 tsp. salt

5 ¾ to 6 ½ cups of all-purpose flour

In a medium-size bowl, sprinkle yeast over milk and stir to dissolve. Let stand for 5 minutes to develop. Add in sugar, egg, butter, and salt and mix well. One cup at a time, add five cups of flour and beat thoroughly each time until flour is incorporated. Add enough of remaining flour to make a soft dough that is slightly sticky.

Turn out onto a lightly floured surface and knead, adding small amounts of flour as necessary to keep dough manageable. Knead for 6 to 8 minutes, until dough is smooth and satiny. Lightly oil the surface of the dough and place it back into rinsed bowl and cover with a clean, dry towel. Allow to rise in a warm place free from drafts until doubled, about 60 minutes.

Punch dough down and shape as directed. For loaf breads, divide dough in half, form into loaves and place in lightly greased 8 ½ x 4 ½ x 2 ½ –inch loaf pans. Cover with a dry cloth and let rise for 30 minutes or until doubled.

Bake in a preheated 375° oven for 35 to 40 minutes or until browned and bottom of loaf sounds hollow when tapped. Remove from pans and let cool on wire racks.

Austrian Povitica

1 batch of Holiday Bread or any
basic white bread recipe

6 eggs

1 ½ to 2 lbs. bacon

1 lb. finely chopped walnuts

2 Tbs. sugar

*This recipe has been in my family for
four generations. My great-grandmother,
Frances Zunic Sardick, brought it to
this country from Austria. You often
see Croatian or Slovenian versions of
this bread (usually called potica) which
use ground walnuts, cream, honey, and
a much sweeter dough rolled into very
thin layers. They are very popular at
Christmas in our area, but I find them
too dry and a bit dull compared to
this beauty, which bakes up as a large,
dramatic loaf with exquisite flavors and
textures. I must admit, my mother makes
this better than I do, but she asks me to
make it anyway!*

Austrian
Povitica

(continued)

Follow instructions for Holiday Bread up to the first rising. While it is rising, chop uncooked bacon into small pieces, and fry until cooked, but not crisp. Drain and set aside. After dough has doubled, punch down and knead for 3 minutes to work out the air bubbles. Roll out onto a large floured cloth to 24 × 30 inches, about ¼-inch thick. Spread bacon bits evenly over dough, then sprinkle the sugar on top. Beat the eggs thoroughly and pour over bacon and dough. Sprinkle chopped walnuts over above ingredients.

Pulling up on the edge of the cloth to help get started, roll up the dough lengthwise jellyroll style. Pull slightly on the dough to get a tight roll, but be careful not to tear holes in the dough. Seal the edges, then make a double coil to form an oval loaf with the two edges tucked into the center. Place in a lightly greased 9 × 13 × 2 ½-inch loaf pan. Cover with a clean cloth and let rise in a warm place until doubled in bulk, about 50 minutes.

Preheat oven to 450°. If any of the egg mixture has leaked out during rising, brush this over the top of the loaf for a glaze. (In any case, get as much of the egg out of the bottom of the pan as possible, or it will cause the bottom crust to burn.) Bake for 10 minutes at 450°, then reduce heat to 350° and bake for about 40 minutes, or until nicely browned. If the bread begins to brown too much on top, cover the loaf lightly with aluminum foil until the last 10 minutes of baking. If your oven doesn't bake evenly, turn the pan around at least once during the baking process to ensure the bread is being baked thoroughly on all sides.

(Adapted from *Breaking Bread with Father Dominic,* 1999)

Ham and Cheese Braid

½ batch of Holiday Bread dough
or any dough enough for one
loaf of bread

1 ½ cups coarsely chopped ham

1 ½ cups sharp Cheddar cheese

1 egg beaten with 1 tablespoon
of water for egg wash
(optional)

This was originally a recipe for a Harvest Braid with chopped apples and walnuts in the filling, but that only works when you have good apples in the fall, so I simplify it for Christmas and Easter. I've made this with every kind of dough you can imagine, from basic white to multigrain to honey oatmeal to rye, and it seems to please my guests every time I serve it.

Ham and Cheese Braid

(continued)

Prepare dough through the first rising. Punch dough down and knead briefly to expel larger air bubbles. On a lightly floured board, roll out to a rectangle about 18 × 10 inches. Prepare filling by combining ham and cheese in a medium-size bowl and tossing to mix. Spread filling lengthwise in the center third of the dough, pressing it together lightly.

Using a sharp knife or a small pizza cutter, cut each outer third of the dough (the part not covered by the filling) into 5 to 10 diagonal strips, cutting from the edge of the dough to about 1 inch from the edge of the filling. Lightly brush strips with water. Fold strips over filling, alternating left and right, being careful not to stretch the dough. Tuck in the ends of the last strips and pinch to seal. Carefully transfer to a lightly greased 13 × 9 × 2-inch baking pan. Cover and let rise in a warm, draft-free place for 30 minutes or until doubled.

If desired, brush surface of loaf with egg wash. Bake in a preheated 375° oven for 30 minutes or until golden brown and the temperature of the filling is at least 160°. Allow to cool on pan for 10 minutes before removing to a wire rack to cool slightly before serving.

(Adapted from *Breaking Bread with Father Dominic*, 1999)

Detail of Window, Saint John the Baptist Church, Bradford, Illinois

Chapter Thirteen

The Lessons Continue

Unlike Easter, with its fifty days of celebration following Easter Sunday, the Christmas season is relatively short. Its brevity reminds us not to try to keep Jesus as a helpless infant for too long. Soon enough, the stories of his infancy and childhood come to an end, and the Holy Child grows up to be a teacher, a miracle worker, a prophet with a challenging message. Above all, he begins to make absolute claims on our attitudes and actions, if we are to claim to be his disciples. Throughout his ministry, he uses the image of bread to continue to teach us lessons about the Kingdom of God.

Immediately after his baptism, Jesus goes out into the wilderness, where he fasts for forty days, and in the midst of his hunger he is tempted by Satan. The tempter says, "If you are the Son of God, command that these stones become loaves of bread" (Matthew 4:3). But Jesus refuses to use his power for his personal gain: "One does not live by bread alone, but by every word that comes forth from the mouth of God" (Matthew 4:4). The child whose birthplace was "the house of bread" insists that we nourish our spirits by breaking open the bread of the scriptures.

As a child, Jesus watched his mother prepare their simple bread and saw in it a powerful prophetic message. Later, he would use the illustration of a woman preparing bread to teach about the nature of his kingdom: "To what shall I compare the kingdom of God? It is like yeast that a woman took and mixed [in] with three measures of wheat flour until the whole batch of dough was leavened" (Luke 13:20-21). To use the image of a woman to represent how God is at work in the world was a radical challenge to his first-century listeners. The parable continues to confront the prejudices of today, the unexamined biases in our own hearts.

When Jesus performs the miracle of the loaves and fishes, the disciples gather twelve baskets of fragments that are left over (Matthew 14:20). This symbolic number indicates that the twelve apostles are equipped to continue his salvific work. We have inherited their mission, their ministry. When we are tempted to complain that we do not have the necessary resources to care for the hungry of our day, we are faced with the gospel story assuring us that God can provide all we need, if we both trust and imitate the generosity of the one who taught us to pray: "Give us today our daily bread" (Matthew 6:11).

Even the wheat we grind for bread offers a symbol of the dying self in order to have a more abundant life: "Amen, amen, I say to you, unless a grain of wheat falls to the ground and dies, it remains just a grain of wheat; but if it dies, it produces much fruit" (John 12:24). If we would produce the fruit of righteousness, if we wish to yield a harvest of holiness and an abundant crop of justice for the poor, we cannot cling to our old lives of selfishness and complacency.

For me, it is the Emmaus story that best illustrates how bread continues to be a powerful symbol of Jesus' message. Luke's gospel reports that on Easter afternoon, two of his disciples are walking from Jerusalem to Emmaus, some seven miles distant. They are discussing the events of the past few days and pondering their meaning. Jesus joins them on the journey, but they are prevented from recognizing him at first. They relate all that they have experienced and heard: Jesus' ministry, his teaching, his passion and death, and the wondrous message from the women that his tomb is empty. Finally, Jesus speaks:

> "Oh, how foolish you are! How slow of heart to
> believe all that the prophets spoke! Was it not
> necessary that the Messiah should suffer these
> things and enter into his glory?" Then beginning
> with Moses and all the prophets, he interpreted
> to them what referred to him in all the scriptures.
> As they approached the village to which they were

going, he gave the impression that he was going on farther. But they urged him, "Stay with us, for it is nearly evening and the day is almost over." So he went in to stay with them. And it happened that, while he was with them at table, he took bread, said the blessing, broke it, and gave it to them. With that their eyes were opened and they recognized him, but he vanished from their sight. Then they said to each other, "Were not our hearts burning [within us] while he spoke to us on the way and opened the scriptures to us?" So they set out at once and returned to Jerusalem where they found gathered together the eleven and those with them who were saying, "The Lord has truly been raised and has appeared to Simon!" Then the two recounted what had taken place on the way and how he was made known to them in the breaking of the bread (Luke 24:25:35).

The gospel passage is a mirror of our own experience of Christian community. We travel together on our journey of faith, and Jesus joins us in ways that we often do not recognize. But our hearts burn within us as he breaks open the bread of his word, the scriptures which continue to inspire and challenge us. And when we gather to break bread together, at last we can recognize the presence of the risen Lord.

Christ is present at our table when we share the daily bread of our common life: the ordinary events of our families, our everyday joys and sorrows, our relationships as husbands and wives, mothers and fathers, children, brothers, sisters, neighbors, and friends. We find him at the table of the Lord's supper, when we share the one bread and the one cup and feel his sacramental Presence drawing us into one body, one spirit in Christ. And when we gather our families and friends to share our holiday feasts, no matter how simple or ordinary or imperfect, he is made known to us in the breaking of the bread.

About the Author

Fr. Dominic Garramone is a priest and monk of Saint Bede Abbey in Peru, Illinois. Following a college education in theatre, he entered the monastery in 1983 and was ordained as a priest in 1992. He describes his culinary education as taking place "between my mother's kitchen and the public library," and he honed his baking skills by providing bread for the twenty-five monks of his community. He is well known to public television viewers for his cooking series *Breaking Bread With Father Dominic*. Father Dom teaches religion and drama at Saint Bede Academy and also enjoys herb gardening and photography. Apart from baking, his favorite part of Christmas preparations is going out on the abbey grounds to collect fresh evergreens.